COUPLE THERAPY

DRAMAS OF LOVE AND SEX

Open University Press
McGraw-Hill Education
McGraw-Hill House
Shoppenhangers Road
Maidenhead
Berkshire
England
SL6 2QL

email: enquiries@openup.co.uk
world wide web: www.openup.co.uk

and Two Penn Plaza, New York, NY 10121–2289, USA

First published 2013

A catalogue record of this book is available from the British Library

ISBN-13: 978-0-33-526336-3 (pb)
ISBN-10: 0-33-526336-4 (pb)
eISBN: 978-0-33-526337-0

Library of Congress Cataloging-in-Publication Data
CIP data applied for

Typesetting and e-book compilations by Fakenham Prepress Solutions, Fakenham, Norfolk NR21 8NN

Fictitious names of companies, products, people, characters and/or data that may be used herein (in case studies or in examples) are not intended to represent any real individual, company, product or event.

COUPLE THERAPY
DRAMAS OF LOVE AND SEX

Barbara Bloomfield & Chris Radley

I would like to thank my husband, Ben, and family Livvy, Zoe and Anna for all their warm support. Many thanks also to our kind editor, Monika Lee, and her team, and all my wonderful colleagues at Relate.

– Barbara Bloomfield

Thank you to Carole, the very therapeutic other half of our own couple, for everything, really.

– Chris Radley

The three stories that follow are fictional and none of the characters or situations are based on real people. Rather, they illustrate some of the issues that couples and families bring to counselling and how a therapist might help their clients to resolve them.

CONTENTS

ABOUT THE AUTHORS

Barbara Bloomfield is a Couples and Family Counsellor and Supervisor with Relate. She is also a former newspaper journalist, BBC radio reporter, producer and an author of several books including *The Relate Guide to Finding Love* (2009).

Chris Radley provides all of the illustrations in this book. He is a freelance creative consultant who has worked chiefly with overseas development and UK social needs charities, a wide range of writing and design and on assignments from political cartooning to graphic novels.

Rudi Dallos is a Professor and Programme Director on the clinical psychology training programme at Plymouth University. His recent book publications include: *Attachment Narrative Therapy* (Open University Press, 2006), *An Introduction to Family Therapy, Third Edition* (OpenUP, 2010) and *Reflective Practice in Psychotherapy and Counselling* (OpenUP, 2009).

INTRODUCTION

Since I was a child I have always loved cartoons and remember how as a Hungarian child refugee it was through cartoons, such as the *Beano*, *Topper*, *Roy of the Rovers* and war comics, that I learnt to understand English. So it was a delight to be invited to collaborate on this graphic book, to write this introduction and also to offer some reflective commentary on the cases with Barbara.

There has been a considerable amount written about counselling and psycho-therapy. I will start by offering one more generalisation to add to the many: Therapy and counselling are multi-sensory activities. This may seem an obvious point, but if one looks at the mountain of textbooks which are predominantly words about therapy with very few pictures you might not realise this.

Therapy and counselling with couples involves being with two people and not just listening to their spoken word but perceiving the dance of their bodies, their gestures, facial expressions, sometimes their touches and even their smell. So, even when descriptions of sessions are presented eloquently and with passion the reader is nevertheless left with an enormous gap in awareness of what this looks like in practice. After all it is often the little things – the quick fleeting smile, the meeting of eyes at a certain point, how a couple's bodies orient to or away from each other – that are so important.

We learn best and most fully when we use all our senses, and likewise couples need to be able to respond at multiple levels to each other. In turn maybe counsellors and therapists chose this activity precisely because it is 'theatrical', in its multi-sensory nature. They do not just want to be academics pondering over words. Most importantly counsellors need to look for where words and actions or gestures are contradictory. This is often a source of deep problems and confusion for couples – 'what are you really saying?', 'you don't seem very sure?', 'we just have sex with no feelings of tenderness', etc. Showing such contradictions between words and bodies needs a visual presentation as well as a verbal one.

Barbara and Chris have done a wonderful job in producing a book which combines the verbal and visual mediums in a highly fascinating and inspiring way. Their skills and craft complement each other: Barbara demonstrates the compassionate skills and aesthetic of counselling in her words and Chris captures the visual aspects with beautiful and sensitive drawings. But this is not just a DVD slowed down with frozen frames. Instead, through the illustration and the following notes and reflections we are invited into the inner worlds of the therapist and the couple.

Through verbal and visual 'thought bubbles' we are guided through the counsellor's inner reflections and clinical formulations. We are able to see how they connect their own personal experiences (counter-transference), draw on psychological and therapeutic theories and connect these with their experience of the couple. Similarly, we are invited to imagine what each person in the couple relationship may be thinking and feeling at different points in the process. The combination of the verbal descriptions and visual images makes this incredibly accessible and compelling. Combining verbal and visual material may also help to consolidate learning and memory of the material in a way that might otherwise not happen so readily.

This book therefore is a valuable resource for a variety of reasons and for a variety of readers: For the layman it can give an accessible insight into the art and science of counselling and also powerful connections with the dilemmas that the couples face. For trainee counsellors it can offer an accessible, thoughtful and inspiring way of learning some aspects of the 'craft'. For trainers it can be an invaluable resource, for example to use in presentations or workshop activities. However, even for experienced trainers and clinicians it can offer clarifications and re-connections with ideas.

Finally, it has been a privilege for me to meet with Barbara and offer some reflections on each of the cases. I hope these are also of interest to the reader. They were intended to capture the vital part that a reflective space offers for couples work. The issues and dynamics can be immensely complex and demanding and counsellors themselves need to feel supported and inspired to think in new ways and to offset any complacency or even compassion fatigue. Make no mistake, working with couples can be very demanding as well as rewarding! Barbara's enthusiasm for critical but constructive self-reflection was impressive and I think the reflective passages capture this. Again these sections may provide a valuable training resource for learning about how to give and receive supervision.

Rudi Dallos

Plymouth, 2013

FOREWORD

As we celebrate our 75th birthday this year, Relate is always searching for fresh, new ways to reach out to those who are in family and relationship distress. We know that many people feel afraid and ashamed about the problems in their lives and a great strength of this book is that it helps to demystify counselling by taking the reader right into the counselling room and alongside three sets of fictional clients.

Chimi and Colston are expecting their first baby. Another couple bring their troubled son to Relate while the final pair, Andrea and Anthony, are struggling with their sex life. I hope these diverse stories will help readers to reflect on their own lives and how they handle challenge and change. I hope readers will go away with the message that it's never too late to resolve relationship unhappiness and that counselling is a warm, supportive and often transforming experience and not the frightening place that some people imagine. We are so privileged that every year some 150,000 people of all ages, backgrounds and sexualities choose to trust us with their intimate lives, and I hope that many more will pick up the phone or contact us online to find out how we can help them once they have read this book.

Couple Therapy: Dramas of Love and Sex provides an engaging and sympathetic visual reference point for what happens in the counselling room. The book is enjoyable and engaging on many levels and it manages to show us how a new perspective can make a difference to a relationship that may seem in crisis, or at a low point.

Throughout our history, Relate has trained thousands of practitioners and today we employ around 1,700 counsellors and therapists. Barbara Bloomfield demonstrates the skill, warmth and understanding that our practitioners possess. I am sure that students of relationship counselling and more experienced practitioners will take away a great deal of learning from this new resource, and I hope that some readers will be inspired to take the first step towards training with Relate to make up our workforce of the future.

Ruth Sutherland, CEO of Relate

THE WARMTH OF STRANGERS

Joining the couple here means finding a common agenda for both of them, rather than highlighting their differences of opinion. Hopefully, I have summed up their joint situation accurately and it may be calming for the couple to hear that I can understand and empathise with the challenges they are facing.

I suppose it's a little more unusual to meet a couple in counselling who seem to be so much in love. But we get the sense that this love is in the 'intense honeymoon phase' perhaps?

Colston takes a risk and blushes when he admits it was Chimi's curves that first attracted him. The sense I'm getting is that Colston is being asked to 'grow himself up' very quickly to a place where he can feel more confident about being a man.

Here is the classic dilemma for a couple who are expecting their first baby. Which one of them is the 'biggest baby,' the one that needs more care and attention until the real baby comes along? Chimi wants her pregnant status to be 'special' but Colston seems to be saying that he needs special looking-after in order to be able to stay with her and manage his anxieties.

And here Colston 'acts out' his anxieties by threatening to leave the session. Perhaps he is testing out the quality of the holding or containment inside the room? Is there a sense that Colston finds it difficult to soothe himself, that he has not learned techniques for dealing with his anxieties in an adult way? I am wondering how Chimi is coping with the special attention being taken away from her and heaped on Colston?

Chimi makes a suggestion that indicates her psychological-mindedness. I'm feeling quite 'parental' towards Colston at this moment, but Chimi seems to be in a more adult place than me with her question about power and control. Colston certainly seems to have taken a powerful central position in the room – does this echo a triangle between him, his mother and his grandmother?

Each client sees another person as having the power at this moment. But I take the opportunity to remind the couple that they are in charge of the sessions and they do have adult choices about continuing the counselling.

Homework tasks are important because they give the clients a focus outside the sessions that will hopefully be productive, interesting and deepen their knowledge of themselves and each other. For this couple, it's a crash course in "Who are you?" Particularly valuable in this mixed-culture couple where race, culture, gender and class differences may be important factors.

A childlike tit-for-tat opening is heightened by tiredness but rather than get bogged down in how each of them has been feeling, I choose to move into looking at their family trees, which I hope will re-energise the couple and broaden the scope of our conversation.

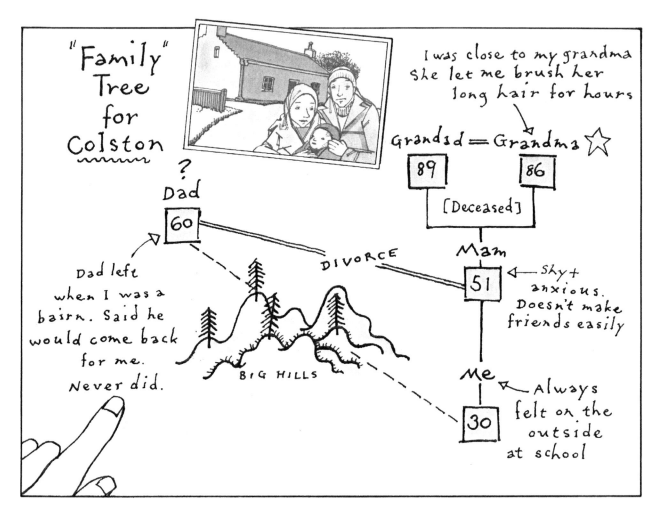

It's easy to see why Colston might fear becoming a father if his own experience of being a small boy was spartan and lonely. We might note the protective factor of his good relationship with his grandmother.

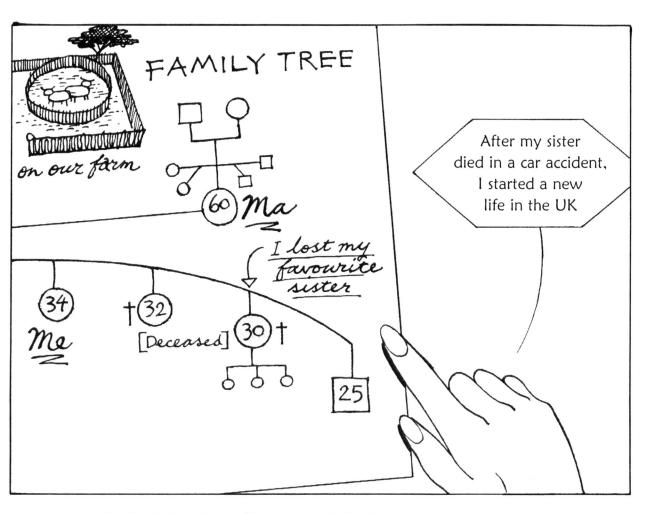

Chimi's upbringing is very different, surrounded by family, and we get a different sense of the emotional tone of her upbringing. Her father had another family elsewhere: how does the black south African context affect her ideas about fatherhood?

I notice Chimi's accepting, almost matter-of-fact tone about her sister's death as something it could be useful to explore further.

More worryingly, with the attention on Chimi's story, Colston has switched off, indicating his lack of ability to hold and contain her feelings. In his discomfort, he commit the communications 'sin' of starting to talking about himself while his partner is trying to say something painful.

I am grateful for having this opportunity to study the pattern of their interaction as I would like to help Colston to develop greater powers of empathy with his partner's feelings.

We rewind and track the rise of his discomfort, leading to a hypothesis that Colston's mother found it difficult to attend to his feelings as a small child, creating an intergenerational pattern. Chimi's guess that her partner feels bad about his inability to relieve her pain is a common difference between men and women: as a generality, women want to 'be listened to', while men wish to 'solve problems.'

It may seem an unusual question, but clients often benefit from asking whether there was a parent, friend or relative who gave them comfort when they were small. A realisation that no-one was able to perform that task is often enlightening. As Rudi Dallos notes in the commentary to this case, Colston was comforted by the sensual brushing of his granny's hair: but there is no suggestion that anyone comforted HIM.

Wise elders and respected relatives who have died can be brought into the room as sources of wisdom. It can be easier to voice someone else's wisdom rather than having to own one's own wisdom! For clients who have faith, it can be useful to ask clients what their God would have to say about a worry or problem?

Colston's remarks about the baby starts to hit the wrong note with Chimi and could lead to an unproductive argument. So I decide to confront him by stepping sideways and he stops playing this particular 'game' of 'who's the father?' If we had let this conversation run, it could have been damaging to the obvious affection between this couple.

I feel it's useful to return to the conversation of last week to see what new ideas are emerging. Colston seems to have been thinking about his father's legacy.

Chimi comes up with an idea from her culture which amazes her partner. Although he rejects her construction, it feels like something is shifting Colston from his childlike yearning for a comforting father figure.

Enactment, according to Jorge Colapinto (1981), is the way: "the therapist introduces disruption in the existent patterns." This couple finds it hard to soothe each other because, when one wants comfort, the other feels resentful as they believe they are more deserving of comfort. Here we see the couple being encouraged to extend their love repertoire. Grooming is a classic bonding behaviour in the animal world, though not so often seen in the counselling room!

Again we see how Colston is attached to being 'the biggest baby' of the family. But Chimi manages not to get activated in this sequence and is able to start to reassure him that there will be enough love to go around.

This is a fragment of a much longer conversation for this couple about sex and love. The bump of her pregnancy is making Colston feel awkward about penetrative sex but there are many other ways he can show his love and they can be intimate.

This feels like a useful exchange about affection and leads to a homework that should be fun and playful but not too threatening of the fragile improvement in the warmth of the relationship.

It's heartening to see that the couple's sexual life is improving. What I want to track is what exactly has made the difference; what are they thinking or doing differently that has led to the improvement?

Colston voices my thought that the couple's relationship, only a few months old, is still based on the passion of first attraction.

Transactional Analysis helps clients to identify times when they are thinking and behaving in a mainly 'parental', an 'adult' or a 'childlike' way. Most of the time, as adults, we will want to be ruled by our adult selves although there are times to enjoy acting like children and times when we need to behave as nurturing or critical parents.

The instability of the parent-child dynamic in a relationship comes when one partner wants to change. In this case, Chimi is likely to find Colston's 'pleading child' manner annoying when she has a baby of her own. Or it could be that Colston will want to be an adult and that Chimi will find it hard not to 'mother' him.

I think the counsellor can sensitively give a voice to those who have died.
Sometimes, after a bereavement, we don't know how to give the dead person a role
in our family. Here, I am saying that Chimi can still keep a connection with her sister
and have a conversation with her.

Using the externalised other is a way of getting clients to 'say the unsayable.' If we had asked Colston or Chimi to 'own' these thoughts for themselves, I am not sure that either of them would have been ready to do so. When we 'say the unsayable', our courage and our words can ring in our ears, long after the counselling has finished.

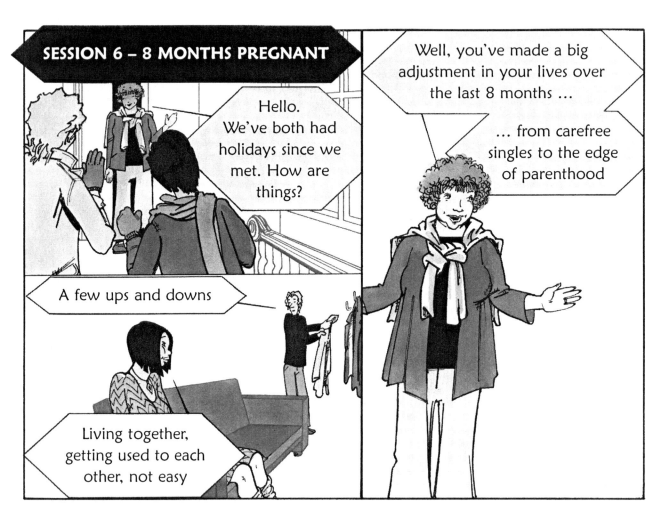

Now that the couple feels more united, and the imminent birth is bringing the sessions to a natural halt, it's time to talk about problem-solving and relapse prevention. Strengthening their sources of support is vital, which is why I intend to open up a conversation about the pros and cons of Colston reconnecting with his family of origin.

I've noticed that many pregnant couples who come for counselling share the experience of isolation: from families of origin, due to geographical distance or as a result of abuse, bereavement or family break up. Typically, such couples may have few close friends and, as the child grows, may find it hard to trust other people – such as babysitters – with their child. I always talk about the importance of support to a new parent.

This reminds me that counselling doesn't always come to a neat ending. Rather, it is 'abandoned' and the couple gets on with their lives.

There are times when common sense means we must be flexible about ending sessions early. Sometimes it's good to be reminded that life doesn't revolve around our counselling room!

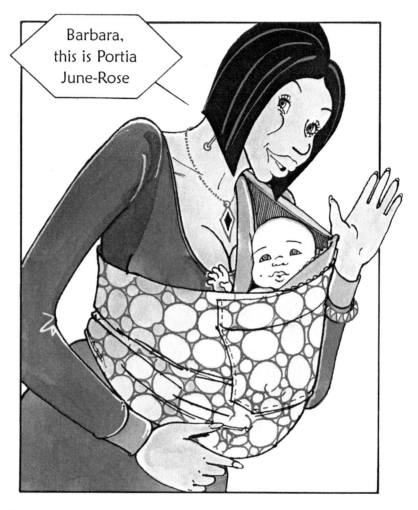

Some couples counsellors prefer not to have young children in the room because they find it distracting. As a family counsellor, unless the conversation is inappropriate for them to hear, I prefer to see how the partners negotiate their couplehood in front of their children – and I enjoy the lightness, warmth and fun that having babies and children in the room brings to the sessions.

THE WARMTH OF STRANGERS

Commentary by Professor Rudi Dallos and Barbara Bloomfield

Chimi, a south African nurse, became pregnant only a few days after meeting Colston, a Scottish man a few years younger than herself. Colston has grave worries about becoming a father and is pulling away from Chimi sexually and emotionally, although the couple says they are 'madly in love.' With the clock ticking to the birth of their child, Chimi and Colston have just a few sessions of counselling in which to prepare themselves for parenthood.

This is a common presentation for couples counsellors, the man who is scared stiff of becoming a father. But also perhaps this is hiding the fact that Chimi has had the emotional trauma of her sister's sudden death in a car accident. Each is asking the question of the other: I want to love you but how much can I entrust my future happiness to you?

Yes, there are a lot of positives for this couple. But Chimi's saying very clearly: "You need to be thinking about me now, it's not just about you." Colston's got to learn how to be a father, so he's got to learn a corrective script

about how to be a father because he has no model for that. He's also got to learn how to be a father who's present and looks after his partner, rather than abandoning her. The last thing he wants is Chimi ending up a sad, depressed woman like his mother.

And he's never had a relationship before, unlike Chimi. When you've got two very different cultures, a Scottish man and an African woman, how much would you attend to difference?

It's important to pay attention to cultural differences but not to be over-organised by them. I sometimes get a bit impatient when therapists get overly cultural because you can lose sight of fundamental relationship dynamics.

So how do YOU balance similarities and difference?

One of our black trainee counsellors did research on the white therapist/black client question and she found there was a conspiracy of silence. She found she would be waiting for the counsellor to mention racial difference, and the overall balance was it didn't get talked about. So the balance is that we should bring it into the room and say, "it's here," because not to talk about race, class, sexuality and other Social Graces can make them an elephant in the room. But we need to do it in a way that doesn't problematise difference and that goes for all the Social Graces.

The thing I've noticed with mixed culture couples is that the stakes are so high if they fall out of love, because if they separate one party will probably want to go back to their country of origin and this is very painful if the other is separated from their children.

I should say I thought the sexual dynamics were a little unusual in this case. To have the woman wanting more sex during pregnancy. Quite often women feel sick or undesirable and they go off it and then men feel resentful and marginalised. How common is it this way around?

I've seen this dynamic often with avoidant attachers like Colston. His strategy is running away from intimacy and I suspect that this couple is in the honeymoon phase of their relationship and there's a high likelihood that the relationship won't last. I suspect Colston's never had sex before and he's 30 years old. You tell me, Rudi, am I right that, for an avoidant attacher, sex is a big deal unless it's casual sex…?

Well yes, unless it's just promiscuous sex, but I still feel it's more likely to be the woman who's gone off it during pregnancy.

Well, their breasts are bigger and that makes them attractive to their partners, but their bellies are bigger too and that makes them scary.

You took a risk in stopping him leaving the room. But he seemed quite childlike, almost like he wanted to be stopped. The trainee might sit there and let him go but you had the gentle, affirming authority to stop him and say 'just stay here a bit longer and you'll be ok' like a kindly aunt, a transitional attachment figure.

 Combing each other's hair was an interesting enactment. They are enacting in front of you some nice physical intimacy and talking about sex. I think you do it very nicely and then you suggest ten touches a day. But perhaps you could explain what led you to take that risk with them and suggest: "Let's treat it as an experiment and see how it goes." I think the flavour of your interaction is optimistic and it's implicit that you won't be disappointed if they don't do it. Using tasks between sessions is important. When Colston gives an example of being comforted it's interesting that he talks

about 'combing his granny's hair' i.e., giving rather than receiving comfort.

 In the room, he feels like a lonely boy.

 He says he feels about five years old…

 …And wants to be at the breast.

 People like that have avoidant attachment strategies and he's already taken a few risks with you in talking about wanting the breast and wanting comfort… it's a good sign that he is able to take these risks with a counsellor.

THE
BURDENED
BOY

A hypothesis is that Karl's behaviour in the room, insistent, noisy but avoiding contact with others in the space, articulates something that the parents do not feel able to say.

Asking who wants or doesn't want to be here acknowledges that some clients may have been 'brought to therapy' by others in the family. It breaks away from a medical model ('What seems to be the problem with little Johnny?') and creates a sense that it is OK for family members to disagree.

A hypothesis here might be that the parents are triangulating in Karl to 'act out' the feelings and conversations they are both avoiding, whatever these may be.

I try to 'join' the couple by suggesting they have both become worried and this is their shared agenda for seeking help. My main aim here is to avoid getting caught in an alliance with one of them which would drive the other away.

It may be too early to try and introduce a creative technique – most clients may expect counselling to be 'a talking cure' and expect to be able to explain their point of view in full. Skills of repeating back what they have said, checking out my understanding and paraphrasing are most useful at this stage.

My objective here is to move away from an unproductive argument but there's a
danger that, if I move too quickly, neither of them will have felt heard or 'contained'
in the room. I think my discomfort with the boy's positioning at the edge of my vision
may have led me to introduce these figures too quickly in an attempt to draw his
interest. A risky strategy?

For the first time, Karl seems interested in the conversation. Seeing his parents 'playing' feels like a bridge to the world of the child. But Peter's awkwardness warns me that it's HE who now feels uncomfortable.

In Lynn Hoffman's words: "Give it a bump and make them jump." I'm trying to expand their understanding of what they are thinking and feeling without scaring them off completely. Developing new ideas about a worry or problem is a good way to get 'air' into the conversation, to reframe and get things in perspective.

Using figures, stones, found objects or coins can be a swift way of finding out a lot about individuals, couples and families because everything they tell us is at the level of story and metaphor which can hold deeper and more mysterious truths than the more rehearsed 'scripts' that we cling to about our lives.

Of course, some part of Peter knows that he has in some way exposed something important about his feelings and so he swiftly defends himself by closing down the conversation.

After taking a risk, we can see here the ways in which family members have moved to defend themselves against pain or exposure by going back to their familiar 'positions.' Perhaps it would have been useful if I had praised this as "looking after and protecting themselves?"

Sometimes young people enjoy being co-opted into a counsellor role that gives them a feeling that what they say is important. This is not one of those occasions!

The relief in the room is palpable as Karl manages to say something as loud and clear as the noisy game he has been playing.

Clients can experience what's called an 'anniversary reaction' to a death or serious loss from the past, when they reach the same age. It's not uncommon for the symptoms to be exactly the same as in the previous loss, though the client may not be 'consciously' aware of this fact.

Developing a genogram or family tree which contains the ages of all the family members is a good way to notice possible anniversary reactions. The idea that we might experience extra fear and worry when we reach the same age as a loved one who has died is something that clients can readily understand and make sense of.

Peter finds it hard to name his emotions. It feels important that Peter's father died at a time they were enjoying themselves – this trauma may have left its mark on his ability to enjoy playing games with Karl. This is a conversation about the 'barriers to having fun' that it could be useful to develop with them.

Jen hits the nail on the head, as is often the case with a family member who observes a 'lightbulb' moment. It is useful to harness the wisdom of other family members who, after all, know their partners much better than the counsellor.

Lightening the mood towards the end of a session (even to the extent of having a brief chat about football) helps this family to make the transition out of the intense, hothouse atmosphere of a counselling room and back into their own lives.

The counselling room is a confidential space and it's sometimes difficult to maintain that privacy and sense of safety if clients want to open up conversations as they leave the building. Suggesting that a subject could be kept for the next session is one way of valuing what they have said without opening up a discussion. To answer Karl's question by reassuring him might have led to another exchange.

THE BURDENED BOY

Commentary by Professor Rudi Dallos and Barbara Bloomfield

Peter and Jen have brought their 10-year-old son, Karl, for family counselling because they are worried that he is depressed and doesn't communicate with them any more. He has brought a noisy computer game into the counselling room and insists on playing it at full blast. The doctors haven't found anything wrong with Karl.

 What strikes me is first where they are sitting in the room.

 Yes, I was a bit slow in noticing that Karl's sitting on the floor in the corner and playing his loud game is his way of saying: "You adults sort this mess out, it's not MY problem!"

 I suppose we would hypothesise that this boy is triangulating some health worries that actually belong to his dad and mum?

 That's what I thought too. I was wondering whether you would use small figures in the way I did?

 Well, Peter gets a bit bothered about these figures and it can be difficult for a trainee when a client says this is nonsense, what's the point? But you go around it and then he engages and becomes very revealing about himself. I tend to use sculpting, coins and stones for people to illuminate how close or how far they feel from each other. I want to focus on process, on closeness and changes in closeness, also in triangulations. What you are doing draws more into the content, and the meaning each person puts on the figures.

 As a writer, I guess I'm more interested in the content of stories. I wonder what Peter means when he says he is paddling his canoe. Could we discuss what, for you, might be the dangers of 'story?'

 Systemic family therapy can become rather bland and we can lose sight of memories from the past, and big parts of Jen and Peter's internal worlds are operating here. If we didn't know this story about the death of Peter's father, it wouldn't make sense...But the figures have revealed some of the hidden story. In my own practice, I would tend to ask: "When you were Karl's age, what did you used to do with your dad?" That might bring out the same information.

 How do you deal with the client who says they can't remember? Particularly when you suspect they are in danger of replicating behaviour or beliefs that they hated in their parents, for example, hitting or bullying?

 I would ask: "If you were able to remember, what would you like to have remembered?" And "Do you think your children will remember how it's been with you?" Sometimes people can't remember because the attachment defences kick in, and you can lessen the stress by suggesting that they might remember something later on. I think your

style is a nice way of getting underneath something because visual material prompts memories at a verbal level and moving things like figures can trigger visual memories from childhood.

 I absolutely agree. But if you're going to do creative techniques you need to bring them in gently and sensitively.

 I noticed that when Jen says she's worried about his heart she sounded very caring and considerate, but I wonder if underneath she's getting a bit pissed off. I'd be thinking of allowing Jen to say she's had enough of this and he should man-up a bit. Because it could feel like Jen's got two children...

 I try to join them both as two adults who are tackling their worries together.

 You join them well by saying: "You both felt hijacked by worries" using an externalising idea that something's come in and made life difficult for you.

 The last thing I want is for them to think I'm on one side rather than the other. So I try and find something they can agree on, in this case, that worries have come in and hijacked the family.

Peter's quite challenging to you, saying you're not a doctor, what do you know and poo-pooing the figures saying "what's this got to do with us?" How would you have dealt with an even bigger challenge?

 Well, that's a question of experience. If I can say with authority: "No, you're quite right, I'm not medically trained ... but I am trained to work with family problems" I think he would accept that. Or I might have said: "I'm using these figures as a way of getting to know you a bit better." One of the nice things about becoming more experienced is having the confidence to suggest active and creative ways of working and also knowing how to deal with the challenges that will inevitably come when we ask people to talk about painful or sensitive things.

MOMMY, DEAREST

The discovery of an affair is perhaps the most upsetting challenge that a committed couple can face. And internet affairs can cause as much pain as real life adultery. However, if a couple is coming to counselling together after an affair, it indicates that they both have strong desire to look at what's gone wrong.

I'm trying to join the couple by reflecting back that they are **both** angry and upset, especially as this has occurred so close to their wedding day. In real life I would be using more reflecting back, paraphrasing and circular questioning to empathise with the extreme stress they must be feeling.

A counsellor needs to be sensitive to the amount of detail that the 'victim' needs to know about the affair. Here, Andrea has obviously become caught up in the unfolding story. But I always caution clients that, once they know all the details, they can never 'un-know' that information and they may be left holding traumatic thoughts.

What I'm feeling here is that the story has certain qualities of a television drama. I'm getting a sense of Andrea's anger, but not of her pain.

From a systemic counsellor's point of view, the suggestion is that the affair has happened **because** the couple wants to stay together but have been unable to talk about a problem in the relationship. The affair becomes a flag for 'the need to talk.' This seems to be what Anthony may be getting at with his comments.

Not being a celebrity myself, I cannot help but be impressed by this couple's closeness to fame and celebrity. Inside, I feel a bit star struck though I try not to show this. But the couple seems relatively low-key about living the glamorous lifestyle.

The couple feels very 'young' and I try to tread the line between promoting their independence and being flexible enough to offer extra sessions because of their wedding deadline. I get the feeling that I could become another powerful mother figure for them, if I'm not careful.

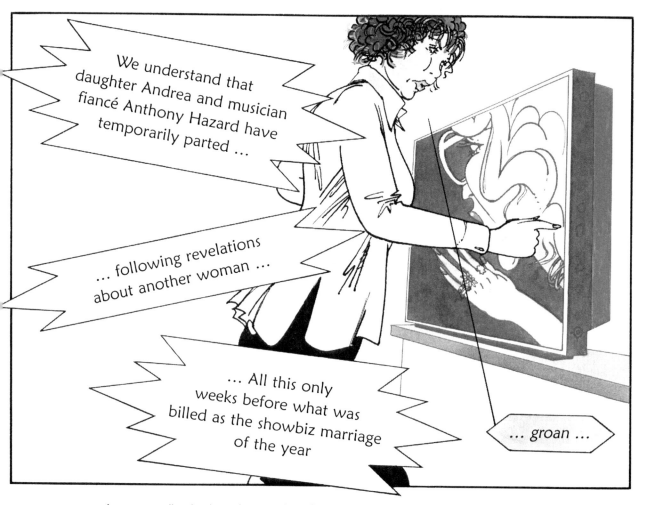

As a counsellor, I value privacy, calm reflection, containment and confidentiality. Therefore, seeing my clients' business spread over the television sends a shiver down my spine as it seems to be the antithesis of the way I work.

We can overestimate couples' abilities to talk quietly and calmly to each other at home. I am not surprised this couple has felt unable to do this. It's really important not to make them feel 'guilty' about their communications difficulties.

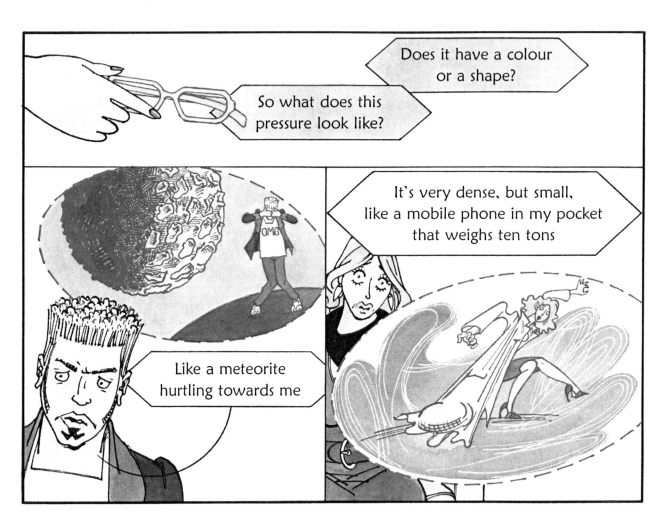

In the systemic way of working, we tend to look at 'problems' as things that 'visit' a person, couple or family, rather than as things that reside inside the individual. If a client can visualise pressure or stress or anger or loneliness, then we may be able to help them to 'move' the problem further away or to shrink it or put it in a box. Some kinds of learners find it useful to enact their problems using their imagination and their body, but others find this way of thinking doesn't suit them.

In the light of the press stories, I'm glad to have the opportunity to restate my confidentiality policy, which I would have given clients before they started counselling. I'm curious that Anthony and Andrea both seem to be worried about what their mother will think.

When clients' loyalty is challenged by their desire for change, we can take the conversation to the level of metaphor where it may be easier to say the unsayable

The clients aren't ready to take this conversation any further at present. I should have slowed down the conversation to a pace that felt more comfortable to them. However, it looks like I've not lost them altogether. I admire the clients for 'voting with their feet.'

It's deeply uncomfortable to be contacted like this outside the counselling room. I'm worried that my confidentiality is being compromised. Also, I'm not sure what information has been shared with Tina. But we have to find ways to deal with these discomforts. I can safely say that I was nearly seduced by celebrity here!

The metaphor of the clean and the dirty comes up again. I guess we all fantasise that 'celebrity life' is clean, sparkly and that 'celebs' don't suffer like normal people. And in some senses, we feel this couple has been packed in cotton-wool and that, with the collapse of their relationship, they may be suffering from dirty feelings for the first time in their lives.

After skirting around the issues and testing out the safety of the counselling room, honest talk can start tumbling out all at once. My job is to try to 'slow down to the pace of wisdom' so that the clients have enough time and space to hear and assimilate the honest conversation without being scared off.

Anthony seems to be trying to get out of the bubble that has held him and Andrea safe but, perhaps, 'sanitised.'

When it comes to sex, clients can feel a great sense of shame and discomfort that they are not doing it (a) right, (b) often enough, (c) passionately enough. We might hypothesise about capitalism's desire to segment markets by making us dissatisfied with our bodies so that we can be sold ever more specialised products that we hope will make us feel 'better!'

Have a look at the systemic theory of Co-ordinated Management of Meaning in Dallos and Draper's *An Introduction to Family Therapy* for further discussion about hierarchies of context and the production of meaning.

The couple has become honest enough to admit that, behind the facade, their lives may be as ordinary and full of ambivalence and challenges, as everyone else.

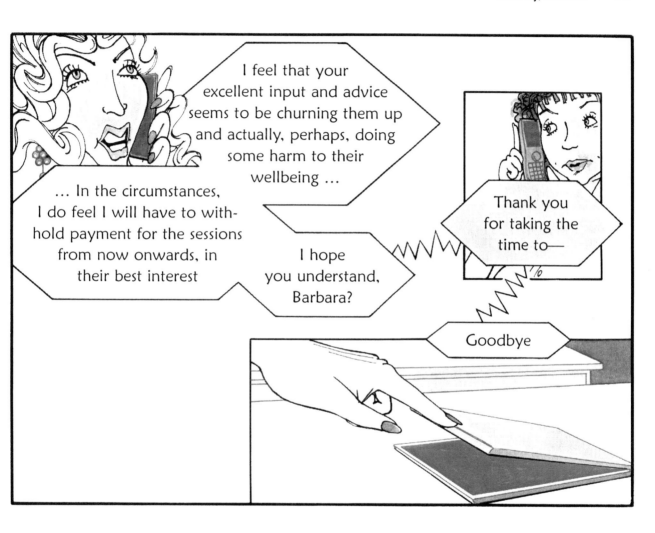

My question turns this into a review session where the couple has a chance to reflect back on the useful and the not so useful. It is always humbling to note that what clients find useful is usually completely different to what I would have predicted. Clients also take away messages they have attributed to me, the counsellor, but I don't remember saying.

A crooked flower crumpled from his pocket symbolises the fragile state of the couple's relationship and the sadness about their cancelled wedding, lost amid the drama.

As their counsellor, I challenge them to start thinking about action that they can take so that something good can come from their painful experience. I'm aware of a tiny prick of irritation that this couple might want ME to organise their future lives.

Big-hearted star, Tina V. has taken pity on the hooker who seduced her daughter's fiancé just weeks before the wedding. Speaking from her Hollywood-style London home, the 65-year-old film star told us exclusively:

"My new mission is to turn Denise's sordid life around. I've always loved helping people and, in fact, have decided to re-train as a counsellor. It can't be that difficult, can it?"

... Will I get to meet Tina V after all?

MOMMY, DEAREST...
Commentary by Professor Rudi Dallos

Andrea and Anthony are weeks away from their marriage but Andrea has caught her fiance using sex chat rooms on the internet. She is furious with him as they appear at Barbara's consulting room for their first counselling session.

 The biggest thing I'm thinking about is the formulation of two young people who are perhaps rather spoiled or pampered but in the midst of luxury, are emotionally poor and living in the mother's shadow. You talk about the influence of this on their lives and then she tries to come in and take over the therapy session. There's a choice point there: whether you try and invite her in or draw a boundary around the two young people. My thought is that's risky: there's a massive risk that they come back united against YOU.

 Yes, they could have left counselling saying: "You're not a very good counsellor!"

 But then you give them the opportunity to have mommy in the sessions...

 ...and they realise the danger that she might take over the sessions.

 I wonder if you'd said "Tina, I appreciate you wanting to be invited and would you mind if I talk to the children first?"

 Funnily enough in a Relate context we wouldn't be allowed to tell Tina that we were seeing her daughter and boyfriend. But as a private counsellor, I certainly could have said that.

 It seems you felt protective about these two children...

 You're calling them children but they're 30 years old!

 I completely feel there's something not right about this too.

They seem to see the value of a separate space.

 But they're little babes in the wood. If they move too quickly away from mother, things might disintegrate and maybe mother is feeling some relief that someone is helping and managing that scary process of young people moving away?

 I feel I had rather taken against the mother and it shows. I denied her any humanity.

 Thinking systemically, if she wants to work with you, I think you should allow that. She's asking you for help.

 Thank you for the reframe: I was seeing the controlling side of Tina but you're saying she's wanting to develop her emotional capacity – it's not just about power and control, it's also about feeling useful and worthy. But, as a counsellor, I'm a bit scared of this high-powered woman coming into MY room and telling ME what to do!

 And when you're feeling like that, it's useful to get some support in the way of supervision or consultation so you're not on your own.

 Very good point.

 When clients say: "We'd like to see you in two days' time." How do we handle that? We don't want them to think it's so serious that they NEED to come in two days' time. We want to give the message, "We have faith that you can last out for a week or two or three..."

 It's hard not to get swept up in their drama when couples say: "Help I'm about to get married and it's all going wrong!" Or, "Help, we're about to have a baby and he wants to leave!"

 How about a counsellor could say: "I've got faith that things won't fall apart in a week but given you've got concerns about the wedding, I'll see you in two days' time." Then we are giving a message conveying that we believe they can manage but we are also holding them...

 Sometimes it's hard to stop clients arguing. How do you think you might halt an argument in the room?

 I think giving them some explanation and asking: "Are you so aroused that you need to carry on your conversation or would it help to take a pause, take a breath so you can feel a bit calmer?" And it doesn't hurt to say that they might NOT find it easy to step back. Almost paradoxically saying: "You might relapse."

I've always been cautious of doing that in case it sounds like I'm suggesting: "This is a good idea, but YOU might not be able to manage it."

My experiences are that it's helpful to put that rider in: "Well, you might find it's not easy.." Your style is conveying an optimism but also something realistic, that you're not expecting miracles overnight.

If I were a counselling client, I'd hate to feel the shame of feeling I'd failed and let down the therapist. I mean, aren't we trying to level the playing field in the room between clients and counsellor?

What were your thoughts when you asked them to think about how they wanted the future to be?

Well, sometimes clients seem to feel the point of counselling is to talk. And it's not! When we think of the Egan three-stage model of counselling – Exploration, Understanding and Action – there can be a danger of not getting into the Action phase.

It's nice the way you ask "...But am I pressurising you?" When they say: "Well, we don't know what to do" and you say: "Well, it's YOUR life and it's all waiting for you." How about opening that up a little further: "Well, would you like me to suggest things for you to do or would you like to use this as a space to open up some ideas?" You say "it's up to you" but then you pick up their distress and their not knowing what to do and you hold that.

Should I have held out a bit longer?

I think this is a lovely example of you showing sensitivity. It would have been head-mistressy to say "Come on you two, try harder!" You keep the relationship warm and caring which is more important than saying "You need to think for yourselves."

So many counsellors can get in a twist about NOT giving advice. But I feel there really can be a place for advice, especially around parenting which none of us get help with.

It's about asking if they would like advice. But I do love saying: "I can give you some advice but you're probably not going to take it."

FURTHER READING

Games People Play: The Psychology of Human Relationships by Eric Berne (2010) London: Penguin Books.

> *This is the first of many, many books on Transactional Analysis (TA), which is a theory of personality which describes how people are structured psychologically. Its best known model, the ego-state model of Parent-Adult-Child interactions, is widely used by counsellors and readily understood by clients.*

Structural family therapy (article) by Jorge Colapinto, in A. Horne and M.Ohlsen (eds.), *Family counseling and therapy* (1982). Itasca, Ill.: Peacock.

> *Enactment is a systemic and family therapy term used to describe how a counsellor gets a couple or family to act out their habitual patterns of relating using their bodies. A key concept in systemic theory is the displacement of the locus of 'pathology' or dysfunction from the individual to the system of transactions that take place **between** the couple or family members. I find this article to be useful in explaining this further.*

An Introduction to Family Therapy: Systemic Theory and Practice, Third Edition by Rudi Dallos and Ros Draper (2010). Maidenhead: Open University Press.

Attachment Narrative Therapy: Integrating Systemic, Narrative and Attachment Approaches by Rudi Dallos (2006). Maidenhead: Open University Press.

> *These two books by Rudi Dallos and Ros Draper offer a readable and thorough approach to the history, concepts and techniques of systemic family therapy.*

Playful Approaches to Serious Problems: Narrative Therapy with Children and Their Families by Jennifer Freeman (1997). London: Norton Professional Books.

Draw on Your Emotions by Margot Sunderland and Phillip Englehart (1997). Milton Keynes: Speechmark Publishing Ltd.

As a creative writer myself, I am always influenced by creative and active ways of promoting relationship health. I believe that many clients improve by 'doing and creating' rather than by talking, as 'doing' imprints change better into the process of counselling. There are many excellent books about creative counselling and I am merely mentioning two that I have particularly enjoyed. The first book by Jennifer Freeman draws on the ethos of the Dulwich Centre in Adelaide, Australia which has a particular interest in narrative therapy and storytelling. Their website is interesting and contains an archive of articles: http://www.dulwichcentre.com.au/michael-white-archive.html.

Draw on Your Emotions is one of many excellent books by Sunderland and Englehart which bring some visual fun back into counselling families and young people.

The Relate Guide to Finding Love by Barbara Bloomfield (2009). London: Vermilion Press.

Offers common sense help and advice on all aspects of dating and relationships. Short, snappy chapters, each containing an exercise plus personal case histories. Many other Relate books are available and Relate's online presence is a mine of information at: www.relate.org.uk

Happy Relationships at Home, Work & Play by Lucy Beresford (2013). Maidenhead: McGraw-Hill Professional.

In this book, psychotherapist and Psychologies agony aunt Lucy Beresford cuts to the chase of how to have harmonious, fulfilling relationships. Whether it's with our partner, our kids, our boss or our mother-in-law, or perhaps most importantly ourselves, Lucy understands the complexities and explains how to fix these relationships with clarity, wisdom and warmth.

Write from the Heart
www.writefromtheheart.co

Val Phillips and I offer creative writing and meditation workshops and events in Bristol, UK, and this is our webpage with more information. We also sell tiny packs of storytelling cards painted by Aaron Sewards – little pieces of inspiration for everyday life. And watch out for our Emergency Poetry Dispensing Machine – inspirational poetry and wisdom coming to your street corner!

Lapidus
www.lapidus.org.uk

Promotes creative writing and reading for well-being, and therapeutic arts for personal development, health and community.